Festive Food Made Simple

John Topham

LAMONA & John Topham

The Perfect Combination

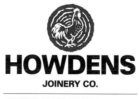

HOWDENS

JOINERY CO.

MAKING SPACE MORE VALUABLE

John Topham

Festive Food Made Simple

In many homes, the festive season starts early in December and lasts right through to *New Year's Day*. So there's a lot of cooking to do – whether it's just for your immediate family, or for visitors from far and wide.

To help make this busy time a little less hectic – and to ensure all your entertaining is a success – this book contains recipes for every occasion. I've included plenty of variety, so you can ring the changes between traditional favourites and new ideas.

I've developed and tested the recipes using Lamona appliances, so I'm sure you'll be delighted with the results. Even if you don't usually do much cooking, I hope these dishes will inspire you to get in the kitchen this Christmas. And if you're a keen cook, you'll find lots of new ways to practise your skills.

Whatever your approach to festive food, the Lamona range offers you choice and versatility – and I can't think of a better way to try out your new appliances than with these festive recipes.

Have a very merry Christmas and a happy new year!

John Topham

Head Chef and owner, The General Tarleton

LAMONA & John Topham
The Perfect Combination

Christmas Day Made Easy

I like to make the cooking on Christmas Day as easy as possible.
And there's no reason why it shouldn't be – after all, it's only like
preparing a Sunday lunch. But because you probably have lots
of other things to do during the morning, it's good to do as much
as you can beforehand – then you can enjoy the day, rather than
being a slave to the stove.

It's all about planning ahead, and the hardest part is the shopping.
Once you've ticked that box, you're well on your way.

I have based my Christmas Day lunch on Menu 1:
Beetroot and Vodka Cured Salmon with Cucumber and Dill Salad.
Roast Turkey Breast with Pine Nut and Pancetta Stuffing, Parmesan
Parsnips and Creamed Celeriac.
Pistachio and Lemon Pavlova.

Feel free to add potatoes and vegetables to your taste.

You can prepare both the starter and meringues for the pavlova in
advance, and the turkey recipe is really easy.

Here is my check list for how you can plan and prepare the meal,
see pages 40–49 for more detail.

23 December	Marinate the salmon.

24 December	Peel and blanch the parsnips, and keep in the fridge. Make the creamed celeriac, leave to cool, and keep in the fridge. Prepare the stuffing balls and, again, put in the fridge. Prepare the turkey, so it's buttered and wrapped in bacon, and keep in the fridge. Prepare the pistachio meringues for the pavlova. Once cool, keep in a sealed container.

25 December

For lunch served at 2pm

10.40am	Remove the turkey breast from the fridge.
11.30am	Pre-heat the oven.
11.45am	Place the turkey in the oven.
12 noon	Prepare the lemon filling for the pavlova and keep in the fridge.
12.45pm	Baste the turkey, and add the stuffing balls.
1pm	Make the cucumber salad for the starter.
1.15pm	Remove the bacon from the turkey, and keep in a warm place. Baste the turkey and turn the stuffing balls.
1.30pm	Warm the creamed celeriac. Bring a pan of chicken stock to the boil.
1.35pm	Remove the turkey from the oven, transfer to a suitable dish and keep in a warm place. Put a tray in the oven for the parsnips, and start to cook. Start to make the gravy.
1.45pm	Slice the salmon and arrange it on plates with the cucumber salad.
1.55pm	Turn the parsnips. Warm the plates. Assemble the pavlova.

Your final checklist before you sit down and enjoy your starter:

      Turkey resting
      Gravy simmering gently
      Parsnips crisping in the oven
      Creamed celeriac warming
      Plates warming

2pm	Enjoy your starter, followed by the main course.

Finally, make the spun sugar decoration for the pavlova.

Store Cupboard Essentials

Store Cupboard Essentials

While you're preparing for the festive period, there are certain kitchen essentials that are always good to have to hand. I've listed the main items here, including some you'll need for the recipes in this book.

Stock up on these, and your Christmas cooking will go much more smoothly.

Dried fruits and nuts:
Raisins
Sultanas
Currants
Cherries
Candied peel
Prunes
Dates
Pine nuts
Mixed nuts
Stem ginger

Spices:
Cinnamon
Cloves
Nutmeg
Star anise
Mixed spice
Juniper
Bay leaves
Peppercorns
Chilli flakes

Oils and vinegars:
Olive oil
Vegetable oil
Rapeseed oil
Truffle oil
Balsamic vinegar
Red and white wine vinegar

Baking:
Flours – plain, self-raising, wholemeal
Sugars – caster, brown, demerara, icing
Golden syrup
Plain chocolate
Gelatine
Yeast
Vanilla pods and essence
Dicarbonate of soda
Baking powder

General:
Mincemeat
Rum butter
Marzipan
Ready made icing
Cake decorating items
Biscuits for cheese
Jams
Marmalade
Honey
Lemon curd
Mustards
Pickles
Breadcrumbs

Festive Gifts

In the run up to Christmas, it's nice to spend a
little time making edible gifts for friends and family.
They are always gratefully received, and there's
something here to suit every taste.

Parmesan Shortbread

Parmesan Shortbread

Savoury shortbread makes a really appetising nibble with drinks – and with a slight kick of cayenne, these biscuits are perfect for warming up chilly festive evenings.

Makes 36 biscuits 20 mins cooking, 45 mins chilling

Ingredients
100g Parmesan cheese, grated
150g plain flour, plus extra for dusting
1 pinch cayenne pepper
1 large egg, beaten
100g unsalted butter

Baking tray, lined with greaseproof paper or baking parchment

1. In a large bowl, mix 75g of the Parmesan with the flour and cayenne pepper. Add the egg and butter, and mix into a dough.

2. On a lightly floured work surface, knead the dough for 30 seconds. Roll it into 2 cylinders, 3cm in diameter, and wrap tightly in cling film so you have 2 smooth tubes. Chill in the fridge for 45 minutes.

3. Pre-heat the oven to 180°C/gas mark 4.

4. Remove the cling film, and slice the dough into 1cm discs. Arrange these on the lined baking tray, and sprinkle with the remaining Parmesan. Bake for 15-20 minutes, until lightly golden.

5. Remove the biscuits from the oven and transfer to a wire rack to cool. Eat them still slightly warm, or let them cool completely and store in an airtight container. They will keep for up to 4-5 days.

Spiced Nut Bars

Spiced Nut Bars

Homemade foodie gifts should always be better than anything you can buy. Whoever receives these intensely tasty nuts will know they definitely haven't come from the supermarket.

Makes 12-18 pieces 10 mins preparation, 1 hour cooking

Ingredients
2 tablespoons soft brown sugar
1 teaspoon cayenne pepper
½ teaspoon smoked paprika
½ teaspoon milled black pepper
1 teaspoon ground cinnamon
2 teaspoons ground sea salt
1 egg white
1 teaspoon water
225g cashew nuts
225g unpeeled almonds
225g pecan nuts

Large baking sheet, lined with non-stick baking parchment

1. Pre-heat the oven to 140°C/gas mark 1.

2. In a small bowl, combine the sugar, cayenne, paprika, black pepper, cinnamon and salt.

3. In a large bowl, whisk the egg white and water until light and frothy. Add the nuts, and mix together. Stir in the sugar and spices, coating the nuts evenly.

4. Line a large baking sheet with baking parchment, and spread the nuts evenly over it. Bake for 50 minutes to 1 hour, until they're crisp and lightly coloured.

5. Let the nuts cool thoroughly, cut into pieces and store in an airtight container. They'll keep for up to 2 weeks.

Biscotti

Biscotti

Italians dunk these twice-baked nutty biscuits in their after-dinner espresso – and I think it's this casual sophistication that makes them such a nice gift.

Makes 24 30 mins preparation, 30 mins cooking, 20 mins cooling

Ingredients
50g hazelnuts, roughly chopped
50g blanched almonds, roughly chopped
50g pistachio nuts
300g plain flour, plus extra to dust
1 teaspoon baking powder
200g caster sugar
1 pinch sea salt
Zest of 1 orange
2 teaspoons fennel seeds
2 eggs, lightly beaten

Non-stick baking sheet

1. Pre-heat the oven to 180°C/gas mark 4.

2. Place all the nuts on a baking sheet, and toast for 8-10 minutes in the oven until they're lightly browned. Leave to cool.

3. Reduce the oven temperature to 160°C/gas mark 3.

4. In a large bowl, combine the flour, baking powder, sugar and salt. Add the nuts, orange zest and fennel seeds, and mix.

5. Gradually add the egg, and mix to form a dough.

6. On a lightly floured surface, divide the dough into 2 equal portions. Roll each one with your hands into a log shape, then gently flatten them to a 4cm width and 2cm height.

7. Place both logs on a non-stick baking sheet. Bake for 20-25 minutes, until they're a pale golden colour and firm to the touch. Remove from the oven and leave to cool for 20 minutes.

8. Cut the logs into 1cm-thick diagonal slices, and lay these flat on the baking sheet. Put back in the oven, and bake for a further 10 minutes or until they're crisp.

9. Transfer the biscotti to a wire rack to cool. They'll keep in an airtight container for up to 10 days.

Chilli and Herb Oil

Flavoured oil is a great gift for anyone who likes cooking – and with all the peppercorns, chillies and herbs, this one looks amazing.

Makes 1 bottle 10 mins preparation, 3 days infusing

Ingredients
1 tablespoon black peppercorns
1 tablespoon white peppercorns
1 tablespoon pink peppercorns
1 tablespoon coriander seeds
6 garlic cloves, peeled
8 small fresh red chillies
4 fresh bay leaves
2 large sprigs fresh rosemary
2 sprigs fresh thyme
Peel of 1 lemon
750ml good-quality olive oil

1 large clear glass bottle with a lid or stopper

1. Sterilise the glass bottle by submerging it in a large container of boiling water for 2 minutes. Take it out and dry. Alternatively, run through your dishwasher on a full cycle.

2. Gently heat a dry frying pan. Add the peppercorns and coriander seeds, and warm through for 1-2 minutes to release their aromas – be careful not to overheat or burn them.

3. Using a funnel, pour the peppercorns and coriander seeds into the bottle. Push in the garlic, chillies, bay leaves, rosemary, thyme and lemon peel, and fill up with olive oil. Seal with the lid or stopper, and leave for 3 days to infuse.

4. This will keep for 6-8 weeks, and can be topped up with more oil once it's opened.

Chilli and Herb Oil

Port-Preserved Cherries

Preserving fruit in alcohol is a lovely winter tradition – and with the cinnamon and orange, this recipe has a particularly festive flavour. Who wouldn't be delighted to receive a gift like this?

Makes 1 jar 20 mins preparation

Ingredients
Juice and grated zest of 1 orange
200ml port
300g light brown sugar
3 star anise
½ cinnamon stick
100ml water
350g fresh cherries, with stalks and stones

1 x 725ml Kilner jar

1. Sterilise the Kilner jar by submerging it in a large container of boiling water for 2 minutes. Take it out and dry. Alternatively, run through your dishwasher on a full cycle.

2. Strain the orange juice into a saucepan. Add the port, sugar, orange zest, star anise, cinnamon and water. Slowly bring this to the boil, stirring occasionally to dissolve the sugar.

3. When the sugar's dissolved, boil the liquid rapidly for 5 minutes, until it becomes syrupy.

4. Wash the cherries, checking their condition, and place them in the Kilner jar. Cover with the syrup and seal. They will keep for 2-3 weeks, as long as they stay sealed, and in a cool place. Once they've been opened, they will keep in the fridge for a month.

Port-Preserved Cherries

Florentines

Florentines

These sticky, fruity chocolate biscuits look as good as they taste – which makes them ideal as a homemade Christmas gift.

Makes 20 20 mins preparation, 10 mins cooking

Ingredients
50g unsalted butter
50g golden syrup
50g demerara sugar
50g plain flour
20 glace cherries, chopped
30g candied peel
30g flaked almonds
100g plain chocolate (70% cocoa solids)

3 baking trays, lined with non-stick baking parchment

1. Pre-heat the oven to 180°C/gas mark 4.

2. Line 3 baking trays with non-stick baking parchment.

3. Gently heat the butter, syrup and sugar in a small pan, until the butter has melted.

4. Remove the pan from the heat. Add the flour, cherries, candied peel and almonds, and stir well.

5. Place teaspoons of the mixture onto the baking trays, leaving plenty of space between each one to let them spread. Bake for 8-10 minutes until golden brown, and leave to cool before transferring to a wire rack.

6. Break the chocolate into small pieces, and melt in a heatproof bowl over a pan of simmering water.

7. Using a palette knife, spread the chocolate over the flat side (the base) of each Florentine. Leave to set, and store in an airtight container. They should keep for 7-8 days.

Family Baking

There's much more to festive baking than Christmas cake. This is a great time of year to have fun making treats for all ages – and to try your hand at some new recipes.

Reindeer Cupcakes

Reindeer Cupcakes

What could be more festive than Santa's reindeer? And when they have pretzels for antlers and chocolate buttons for ears, they'll be the star of the show at every party!

Makes 12 30 mins preparation, 25 mins cooking

Ingredients
275g caster sugar
200ml sunflower oil
4 medium eggs
300g carrot, grated
225g wholemeal flour
2 teaspoons baking powder
1 teaspoon ground cinnamon
1 teaspoon mixed spice

For the icing
200g dark chocolate
100ml double cream
50g icing sugar

For decorating
Mini chocolate buttons (ears)
M&M's sweets (nose)
Pretzels (antlers)
Mini marshmallows (eyes)
Mini amaretti biscuits (snout)

Cupcake tin
Cupcake cases

1. Pre heat the oven to 180°C/gas mark 4.

2. Line the cupcake tin with cupcake cases.

3. Beat the sugar, oil and eggs in a mixing bowl until smooth, and then stir in the carrot.

4. In a separate bowl, mix the flour, baking powder, cinnamon and mixed spice. Add this to the carrot mixture and stir well.

5. Fill each cupcake case to two thirds full, and bake in the oven for 25 minutes, until the cakes are golden.

6. Remove from the oven and leave to cool.

To make the icing and decorate

1. Melt the dark chocolate in a heatproof bowl over a pan of barely simmering water. When it's melted, take off the heat, and stir in the double cream. Sift in the icing sugar and mix well.

2. Top each cake with a layer of the icing, saving some to finish the reindeer eyes, and to stick the nose to the snout.

3. Using the decorating ingredients as listed above, design each reindeer.

The photo shows you one way to do it – but feel free to let your creativity run wild!

Stem Ginger Christmas Tree Biscuits

I love the flavours of ginger and cinnamon at Christmas time. So although I'll be hanging these biscuits on my tree, I'm not sure how long they'll stay there!

Makes 12 large biscuits 45 mins preparation, 15 mins cooking, 1 hour chilling

Ingredients
100g softened unsalted butter
75g dark brown sugar
2 tablespoons golden syrup
1 medium egg, beaten
225g plain flour
1 teaspoon ground ginger
½ teaspoon ground cinnamon
½ teaspoon baking powder
1 pinch salt
75g stem ginger, roughly chopped

For the icing
500g icing sugar
Juice of 2 lemons

Christmas-themed biscuit cutter
Baking sheet, lined with greaseproof paper
or baking parchment
Small piping bag and nozzle
String or ribbon

1. Whisk the butter and sugar until light and fluffy. Add the syrup, and then gradually add the egg.

2. In a separate bowl, mix the flour, ginger, cinnamon, baking powder and a pinch of salt. Sift this into the butter mixture and stir.

3. Fold in the stem ginger and bring the mixture together with your hands.

4. Roll out the dough between 2 sheets of cling film, until it's the thickness of a pound coin. Place on a baking tray and chill in the fridge for an hour.

5. Pre-heat the oven to 160°C/gas mark 3.

6. Remove the cling film from the dough and, using your cutter, cut out the biscuits. Transfer them to your lined baking sheet, and bake for 12-15 minutes, until golden brown.

7. While hot, use the nib of a small piping nozzle to cut a hole in the corner of each biscuit, and then leave to cool.

To make the icing and decorate

1. Sift the icing sugar into a bowl, and whisk in the lemon juice until you have a smooth paste of piping consistency.

2. Spoon the icing into a piping bag and decorate the biscuits to your design.

3. Leave the icing to set. Then tie string or ribbon through the hole of each biscuit, so they can hang on the Christmas tree.

Stem Ginger Christmas Tree Biscuits

Chocolate and Black Cherry Roulade

Serves 8-10 40 mins preparation, 25 mins cooking

Ingredients

6 large eggs, separated
150g caster sugar
50g cocoa powder
Icing sugar to dust
390g jar black cherries soaked in Kirsch
250ml double cream

For the mousse

250g dark chocolate (70% cocoa solids), broken into pieces
3 large eggs, separated

Electric mixer
30cm x 18cm, 2.5cm deep baking tray

1. Pre-heat the oven to 180°C/gas mark 4.

2. Oil the baking tray, and line with baking parchment.

To make the mousse

1. In a heatproof bowl, melt the chocolate over a pan of gently simmering water. When it's melted, remove from the heat and beat with a spoon until smooth.

2. Whisk the 3 egg yolks, and mix into the chocolate.

3. In a separate bowl, whisk the 3 egg whites until stiff, and fold into the chocolate mixture until blended. Keep the mousse in the fridge.

To make the roulade

1. In a large bowl, whisk the egg yolks and caster sugar until they thicken slightly and appear lighter in colour. Stir in the cocoa powder until the mixture becomes smooth.

2. Using an electric mixer, whisk the egg whites to soft peaks. With a large balloon whisk, fold the whites into the chocolate mixture and pour this into the baking tray. Bake for 20-25 minutes, until springy to the touch. Remove from the oven and leave to cool slightly in the tray.

3. Heavily dust a large sheet of baking parchment with icing sugar, and turn the slightly warm cake onto it. Carefully peel off the baking parchment.

4. Spread the chocolate mousse evenly all over the cake, and dot with the cherries. Whip the cream to soft peaks, and spread it on top of the mousse.

5. Finally, gently roll up the cake to make a log shape, using the dusted sheet of baking parchment to help. Dust the roulade with extra icing sugar to serve.

Chocolate and Black Cherry Roulade

Brandy Snaps

Part biscuit, part dessert, these teatime treats have a slightly retro feel that's just right for Christmas time. Kids love the sticky sweetness, and the addition of stem ginger to the filling adds a little more flavour and texture for the grown-ups.

Makes 24 15 mins preparation, 1 hour cooking

Ingredients
50g golden syrup
50g unsalted butter
50g demerara sugar
50g plain flour
1 teaspoon ground ginger
½ teaspoon lemon juice
Vegetable oil to grease

For the filling
300ml whipping cream
30g stem ginger, chopped

2 baking trays, lined with
non-stick baking parchment
4 wooden spoons
Piping bag

1. Pre-heat the oven to 160°C/gas mark 3.

2. Line 2 baking trays with non-stick baking parchment.

3. Place the syrup, butter and sugar in a small pan, and heat gently until the butter has melted.

4. Take the pan off the heat, and sift the flour and ginger into it. Stir the mixture until smooth, add the lemon juice, and mix thoroughly.

5. Place 4 teaspoons of the mixture on each baking tray, spacing them out widely to let them spread.

6. Put 1 baking tray in the oven, and bake for 8-10 minutes, until you have 4 golden brandy snaps.

7. Remove from the oven, and let them cool for a minute.

8. Rub the handles of 4 wooden spoons with a little oil. Quickly flip each brandy snap off the baking tray and roll it around the handle.

9. Leave the brandy snaps to set on a wire rack, and slide them off the spoons when they're cold. If the brandy snaps have cooled too quickly, and won't roll around the spoon handles, put the tray back in the oven to warm through again, and then repeat as above.

10. Put the second tray in the oven, and repeat as above.

11. Repeat from step 5, until you have 24 brandy snaps. Store in an airtight container – they should keep for 4-5 days.

12. When you're ready to serve, whip the cream into soft peaks, and fold in the stem ginger. Place this in a piping bag and fill each brandy snap.

Mince Pies with Streusel Topping

Mince Pies with Streusel Topping

Makes 24 30 mins preparation, 20 mins cooking, 1 hour chilling

Ingredients
75g icing sugar, plus extra to dust
150g softened unsalted butter, plus extra
to grease the pie trays
1 egg, beaten
Juice and grated zest of ½ orange
250g plain flour, plus extra to dust
1 pinch sea salt
25g ground almonds
400g jar good-quality mincemeat

For the streusel topping
50g plain flour
30g softened unsalted butter
¼ teaspoon ground cinnamon
25g demerara sugar
25g lightly toasted hazelnuts, chopped

Electric mixer
7.5cm fluted pastry cutter
2 x 12-hole pie trays

1. Using an electric mixer, blend the sugar and butter until light and fluffy. Slowly add the egg, a little at a time, followed by the orange juice and zest.

2. Sift the flour into a separate bowl, add the salt and ground almonds, and mix together.

3. With the mixer on a low speed, gradually add the flour mixture to the sugar and butter, to form a soft dough.

4. Wrap the dough in cling film, and chill in the fridge for 40 minutes.

5. Roll out the dough on a cool, lightly floured work surface, until it's 3mm thick. Use a 7.5cm fluted pastry cutter to cut out 24 bases.

6. Lightly grease the pie trays with the extra butter. Place the bases in the tray, and fill each one with a teaspoon of mincemeat. Chill in the fridge for 20 minutes.

To make the streusel topping and finish the pies

1. Pre-heat the oven to 190°C/gas mark 5.

2. Sift the flour into a bowl, and rub in the butter until the mixture looks like fine crumbs.

3. Add the cinnamon and sugar, and continue to rub until the mixture forms little nuggets. Then stir in the hazelnuts.

4. Spoon a heaped teaspoon of the streusel mix over each pie, and bake for 20 minutes until golden.

5. Leave the pies to cool in the tray for 5 minutes, then place on a wire rack to cool fully. Dust with icing sugar to serve.

Sour Cherry, Almond and Pistachio Stollen

Sour Cherry, Almond and Pistachio Stollen

Makes 1 loaf 30 mins preparation, 50 mins cooking, 1 hour 30 mins proving

Ingredients

300g strong white bread flour, plus extra to dust
1 pinch sea salt
100g softened unsalted butter, plus extra to grease
50g caster sugar
7g sachet instant dried yeast
Zest of 1 lemon
Zest of 1 orange
100g dried sour cherries
75g whole blanched almonds, roughly chopped

75g pistachio nuts
150ml milk
½ teaspoon vegetable oil to grease
125g marzipan

For the icing
100g icing sugar
3-4 tablespoons lemon juice

Rolling pin
Large baking sheet

1. Sift the flour and salt into a large bowl. Add the butter, and using your fingers rub into the flour until the mixture resembles fine crumbs.

2. Mix in the sugar, yeast, lemon and orange zest, cherries, almonds and pistachio nuts.

3. Gently warm the milk in a small pan, until tepid.

4. Make a well in the centre of the mixture. Gradually pour in the milk, and mix to form a soft dough.

5. Dust a work surface with a little flour, and knead the dough for 10 minutes until shiny and elastic.

6. Lightly oil a glass bowl, add the dough and cover with cling film. Leave in a warm place for 1 hour, until it has doubled in size.

7. Use your fist to knock back the dough, then turn it onto a floured work surface. Using a rolling pin, roll into a rectangle, about 20cm x 10cm.

8. Roll the marzipan into a long sausage shape, a little shorter than the length of the dough. Place on top of the dough, about three quarters of the way across, so that when you fold the dough over the top, the marzipan is in the centre. Press the dough at the ends and along the seam to seal it.

9. Lightly grease a large baking sheet and place the stollen on it. Cover with lightly greased cling film, and leave to rise in a warm place for 30 minutes.

10. Pre-heat the oven to 160°C/gas mark 3.

11. Bake the stollen for 50 minutes until golden. Transfer to a clean tea towel, wrap and leave to cool.

12. Mix the icing sugar and lemon juice until smooth and shiny. Spread the icing over the stollen, and let it set before slicing and serving.

Festive Menus

Over the festive period, many of us have to entertain guests for more than just Christmas Day. To help you give every meal a sense of occasion, I've put together 4 menus you can mix and match, combining new ideas with some twists on traditional favourites.

Beetroot and Vodka Cured Salmon with Cucumber and Dill Salad

Beetroot and Vodka Cured Salmon with Cucumber and Dill Salad

Curing fish at home may sound ambitious, but it's actually very simple. And, because of the curing time, you can do the preparation well in advance – making this impressive starter virtually stress-free.

Serves 8 15 mins preparation, 36 hours curing

Ingredients
500g salmon fillet, pin boned
1 teaspoon black peppercorns
1 dessertspoon coriander seeds
1 dessertspoon fennel seeds
1 tablespoon caster sugar
3 tablespoons coarse sea salt
Zest of ½ lemon
2 medium beetroot, peeled and grated
3 tablespoons vodka

For the cucumber and dill salad
1 cucumber, peeled, de-seeded and cut into batons
1 dessertspoon sea salt
1 tablespoon caster sugar
3 tablespoons white wine vinegar
3 sprigs dill, finely chopped

2 x baking trays
Pestle and mortar

1. Lay large sheets of cling film loosely over a baking tray. Place the salmon fillet on top, skin side down.

2. In a dry frying pan over a medium heat, lightly toast the black peppercorns, coriander seeds and fennel seeds for 2 minutes. Crush them gently in a pestle and mortar, and put them in a bowl with the sugar, salt and lemon zest, and mix together.

3. Stir in the beetroot and vodka, and spread the mixture evenly over the salmon fillet.

4. Lift the sides of the cling film, and wrap tightly around the salmon.

5. Place another baking tray on top of the salmon, along with a few cans of food to weigh it down. Keep in the fridge for 36 hours.

6. Unwrap the salmon and discard the marinade. Rinse the fish under cold water, pat dry with kitchen paper to remove any moisture, and re-wrap in cling film. Keep in the fridge until you need it – for up to 5 days.

7. To make the salad, place the cucumber batons in a colander, sprinkle with salt, and leave to drain for 10 minutes. Rinse off the salt under cold water and pat the cucumber dry with kitchen paper. In a small bowl, mix the sugar and vinegar until dissolved, add the cucumber and dill, and stir together.

8. Remove the cured salmon from the cling film, and thinly slice it away from the skin. Serve with the cucumber and dill salad.

Roast Turkey Breast with Pine Nut and Pancetta Stuffing, Parmesan Parsnips and Creamed Celeriac

42

Roast Turkey Breast with Pine Nut and Pancetta Stuffing, Parmesan Parsnips and Creamed Celeriac

If you find the idea of dealing with a whole turkey a little daunting, try this version of the Christmas roast. You'll be surprised how much meat is on the breast – and the stuffing, parsnips and celeriac complete the feast beautifully.

Serves 10-12 35 mins preparation, 1 hour 50 mins cooking

Ingredients
2kg whole turkey breast
50g softened unsalted butter
Milled black pepper
18 rashers streaky bacon or pancetta, thinly sliced
1 tablespoon olive oil

For the stuffing
1 tablespoon olive oil
25g unsalted butter
2 medium onions, peeled and finely diced
1 teaspoon fennel seeds
3 garlic cloves, crushed
140g pancetta, diced
20g parsley, chopped
10g fresh thyme leaves, picked
20g fresh sage, chopped
Zest of 1 lemon
50g pine nuts, toasted
Sea salt and milled black pepper
150g coarse breadcrumbs
400g sausage meat
1 egg, beaten

For the gravy
2 tablespoons plain flour
300ml white wine
500ml chicken stock

For the parmesan parsnips
2.5kg parsnips
150g plain flour
75g Parmesan cheese, finely grated
Sea salt and milled black pepper
3 tablespoons vegetable oil
20g unsalted butter

For the creamed celeriac
1 large celeriac
1 garlic clove, peeled and sliced
3 shallots, peeled and diced
200ml double cream
Sea salt and milled black pepper

2 large roasting tins
Food processor

To prepare the turkey breast

You can do this stage the day before you cook the dish.

1. Place the turkey breast on a chopping board, smear the butter evenly all over, and season with black pepper.

2. Arrange the bacon or pancetta in a lattice pattern over the skin. Wrap the breast tightly in cling film, and put in the fridge.

To make the stuffing

You can also make this a day in advance.

1. In a large frying pan, heat the olive oil and butter until it starts foaming. Add the onions, and cook for 5 minutes until soft.

2. Add the fennel seeds and garlic, and cook gently for a further 5 minutes.

3. Tip the onions, fennel seeds and garlic into a bowl. Increase the heat and cook the pancetta for 5 minutes, until golden and crispy. Add to the ingredients in the bowl, and leave to cool completely.

4. When the onion and pancetta mixture is cool, add the parsley, thyme, sage, lemon zest and pine nuts. Season with salt and pepper, and mix well. Add the breadcrumbs, sausage meat and egg, and bind together.

5. With wet hands, shape the stuffing into balls, about the size of a golf ball. Keep covered in the fridge until you need them.

To cook the turkey

1. Remove the turkey breast from the fridge, and take off the cling film. Leave for 40 minutes to let it reach room temperature.

2. Pre-heat the oven to 190°C/gas mark 5.

3. Rub the base of a large roasting tin with the olive oil. Put the turkey in, and roast for 1 hour.

4. Remove from the oven, and baste the turkey in the juices. Add the stuffing balls, rolling them lightly in the cooking juices. Put back in the oven, and cook for a further 30 minutes.

5. Take it out of the oven again, and give the stuffing balls a stir. At this stage you can take the bacon or pancetta off the turkey breast and keep to one side in a warm place, so the turkey crisps.

6. Increase the oven to 200°C/gas mark 6. Baste the turkey once more, and return to the oven for a further 20 minutes.

7. Remove from the oven, lift the turkey and stuffing balls onto a serving dish, and rest in a warm place for 10-15 minutes. Keep the tin and juices to make the gravy.

To make the gravy

1. Remove any excess fat from the roasting tin. Mix 2 tablespoons of the juices with the plain flour, making a smooth paste.

2. Place the tin over a high heat, add the white wine and de-glaze the pan, using a wooden spoon to loosen any sediment.

3. Reduce the volume by half, then add the chicken stock. Bring to the boil and whisk in the flour paste to thicken.

4. Pass the gravy through a sieve into a saucepan, and simmer gently while you finish the final stages.

To make the Parmesan parsnips

1. Pre-heat the oven to 200°C/gas mark 6.

2. Peel the parsnips and cut lengthways into quarters. Remove any woody core, and cut across into even pieces.

3. Bring a large pan of salted water to the boil. Add the parsnips, bring back to the boil and simmer for 6-7 minutes. Drain the parsnips in a colander and leave to stand for a few minutes.

4. In a large bowl, mix the flour, Parmesan, salt and pepper. Tip a few parsnips at a time into the flour mixture, and shake to get an even coating. Repeat with the remaining parsnips.

5. Place a large roasting tin in the oven. When it's hot, add the vegetable oil and butter, and swirl around until the butter has melted. Add the parsnips, basting them in the oil and butter.

6. Return the tin to the oven, and cook the parsnips for 20 minutes. Turn the parsnips over, and drain any surplus fat. Continue to cook for 15 minutes, until they're crisp and golden.

To make the creamed celeriac

1. Peel the celeriac, and cut into even-sized pieces – about 3cm cubes.

2. Put in a pan with the garlic and shallots. Cover with cold water, and bring to the boil. Turn the heat down to a simmer and cook for 20-25 minutes, until the celeriac is tender. Drain in a colander, and leave to stand for a few minutes.

3. Add the cream to the pan, and bring to the boil. Add the celeriac, garlic and shallots, bring the cream back to the boil and simmer gently for 10 minutes.

4. Pour the cream and celeriac into a food processor, and purée until smooth and velvety. Check the seasoning, adding salt and pepper if necessary. Place in a serving dish, and keep in a warm place until you need it.

To finish and serve

1. When the turkey has rested, and you have all the vegetables ready, serve with the stuffing balls, crisp bacon or pancetta, and gravy.

Pistachio and Lemon Pavlova

Pistachio and Lemon Pavlova

Pavlova always impresses at a dinner party – and this one has the extra crunch of pistachios in the meringue. To make it even more of a show-stopper, you can decorate it with spun sugar. Don't worry, this is easier than it looks!

Serves 8 30 mins preparation, 1 hour 30 mins cooking

Ingredients
6 eggs, separated
1 pinch salt
450g caster sugar
2 teaspoons cornflour
2 teaspoons white wine vinegar
50g pistachio nuts, crushed
Juice of 2 lemons
Zest of 1 lemon
300ml double cream
2 leaves gelatine

For the spun sugar (optional)
200g caster sugar
80ml water

Electric mixer
3 flat baking trays, lined with non-stick baking parchment

1. Pre-heat the oven to 120°C/gas mark ½.

2. Using an electric mixer, beat the egg whites until foamy. Then add the salt, and keep mixing until soft peaks form.

3. Gradually add 300g of the caster sugar, a little at a time, continuing to mix until firm and glossy. Fold in the cornflour and white wine vinegar followed by the pistachios, using a metal spoon.

4. Divide the mixture between the trays, and use a pallet knife to create identical sized discs. Use a fork to pull up the meringue into peaks.

5. Place the trays in the oven and bake for 1 hour 30 minutes. Turn the oven off and let the meringues cool inside.

6. In a heatproof bowl, mix the egg yolks with the remaining 150g of caster sugar, the lemon juice and zest, and 150ml of the cream. Place the bowl over a pan of boiling water, and whisk the mixture for 10-12 minutes until thickened – you should be able to see the ribbons left from the whisk trail.

7. Remove the bowl from the heat, and carry on whisking for another 2 minutes while the mixture cools.

8. Soak the gelatine in cold water for 2 minutes, remove and squeeze out any excess water. Whisk into the lemon mixture, then leave to cool for 20 minutes.

9. Whisk the remaining cream into stiff peaks, and fold into the lemon mixture. Keep this in the fridge until you need it.

10. To assemble the pavlova, divide the lemon mixture over 2 of the meringue discs, spreading it to the edges. Layer one disc on top of the other, and place the third plain meringue on top.

To make the spun sugar (optional)

If you want to decorate your pavlova, make the spun sugar just before serving.

1. In a large, heavy-based saucepan, warm the sugar and water over a medium heat, stirring until the sugar dissolves.

2. Remove the spoon, increase the heat, and cook the caramel until it turns an amber golden colour. Take it off the heat and place on a trivet to cool slightly.

3. Place a large sheet of baking parchment on a work surface. Dip a fork into the caramel, then quickly whip it back and forth over the parchment. Keep doing this until you have a large dome of spun sugar.

4. Carefully place the sugar dome on top of the pavlova, and serve.

Jerusalem Artichoke Soup finished with Truffle Oil

A classic winter vegetable, the Jerusalem artichoke has a distinctively sweet, nutty flavour that adds real character to this luxurious soup.

Serves 4 15 mins preparation, 30 mins cooking

Ingredients
500g Jerusalem artichokes
20g butter
1 onion, peeled and finely chopped
1 leek, washed and finely chopped
100g button mushrooms, sliced
1 litre water
1 vegetable stock cube
125ml double cream
Sea salt and milled black pepper
Truffle oil (optional)
1 tablespoon chives, chopped

Food processor

1. Wash and peel the artichokes, and chop into 2cm cubes.

2. Heat a large, heavy-based pan. Add the butter and onion, and cook for 4-5 minutes, until the onion starts to soften.

3. Add the leeks, mushrooms and artichokes, stir well and cook gently for 10 minutes.

4. Boil the water, add the stock cube, whisk together and pour onto the vegetables. Bring to the boil, reduce the heat and simmer for 20 minutes, until the artichokes are soft.

5. Ladle the soup into a food processor and blend until smooth. Return to the pan, add the cream, and bring back to a gentle simmer. Check the seasoning, adding salt and pepper if necessary.

6. Pour the soup into bowls, and drizzle with truffle oil if you're using it. Sprinkle with black pepper and chives to serve.

Jerusalem Artichoke Soup finished with Truffle Oil

Salmon Wellington

After all the hearty meat dishes of the festive season, salmon can make a refreshing change. Here, with a creamy, nutty, watercress filling, and wrapped in puff pastry, it's a superb centrepiece for your lunch or dinner party.

Serves 6 25 mins preparation, 40 mins cooking, 40 mins chilling

Ingredients

1 bunch watercress
50g toasted pine nuts
25g sultanas
Zest of 1 lemon
1 teaspoon creamed horseradish sauce
100ml crème fraîche
Sea salt and milled black pepper
1kg salmon fillet, boned and skinned
200g smoked salmon, sliced
1 tablespoon plain flour for dusting

500g ready-made puff pastry
1 egg, beaten
½ teaspoon sea salt
1 teaspoon vegetable oil

To Serve

Seasonal vegetables, or
mixed salad leaves

Non-stick baking tray

1. Remove and discard the watercress stalks and chop the leaves roughly. Place in a bowl with the pine nuts, sultanas, lemon zest, horseradish sauce and crème fraîche. Season with a little salt and pepper, and mix together.

2. Cut a slit in the salmon fillet to form a pocket along the length. Fill this with the watercress mixture, and then lay the slices of smoked salmon over the incision to help keep the filling secure.

3. On a floured surface, roll the pastry to a thickness of 3mm, and then trim to a 36cm x 42cm rectangle.

4. Place the salmon on top of the pastry, to one side, leaving a small border. Brush the edges of the pastry with some of the beaten egg, and fold over the top of the salmon. Trim the edges and crimp together to seal.

5. Place the salmon parcel on a tray, and chill in the fridge for 40 minutes.

6. Pre-heat the oven to 200°C/gas mark 6.

7. Place a non-stick baking tray in the oven for 5 minutes to heat.

8. Remove the salmon parcel from the fridge, brush with the remaining beaten egg, and sprinkle with sea salt.

9. Take the hot baking tray out of the oven, and brush with vegetable oil. Carefully place the parcel on top, and bake for 35-40 minutes until golden.

10. Lift onto a serving plate, and slice. Serve with seasonal vegetables or mixed salad leaves.

Salmon Wellington

Iced Praline Nougatine

With the satisfying crunch of sticky praline, this light, creamy frozen dessert takes homemade ice cream to a whole new level.

Serves 12 25 mins preparation, 12 hours setting

Ingredients
425g caster sugar
80g hazelnuts, shelled and roughly chopped
Vegetable oil to grease
6 egg whites
450ml double cream
250g fresh raspberries
12 sprigs mint

Terrine or loaf tin
Baking tray
Food processor

1. Line a terrine or loaf tin with greaseproof paper and put in the freezer.

2. In a heavy-bottomed saucepan, heat 150g of the sugar until it melts and turns a golden caramel colour. Take off the heat and stir in the hazelnuts. Pour the mixture onto a lightly oiled tray to set into praline.

3. When the praline is hard, crush into small pieces.

4. Whip the egg whites to soft peaks. Gradually add the remaining sugar, beating for 3-4 seconds between each addition, until you have a stiff meringue.

5. In a separate bowl, whip the cream into stiff peaks.

6. Fold the cream and crushed praline into the meringue, and pour this into the chilled, lined terrine tin. Put in the freezer and leave to set for at least 12 hours. You can keep it in the freezer for up to 2 weeks, as long as it's covered.

7. To serve, remove the nougatine from the freezer. Keep enough raspberries for decoration and purée the rest in a food processor. Pass them through a sieve into a small bowl, making a smooth coulis. Cut slices of the nougatine, and serve each one with a pool of the raspberry coulis, a couple of raspberries and a sprig of mint.

Iced Praline Nougatine

Crayfish and Avocado Cocktail

Crayfish and Avocado Cocktail

So much more appealing than a standard seafood cocktail, this creamy, tangy starter will set the mood for any festive dinner or lunch.

Serves 4 15 mins preparation

Ingredients
1 ripe avocado
Juice of 2 limes
2 tablespoons crème fraîche
3 tablespoons mayonnaise
1 tablespoon sweet chilli jam
½ iceberg lettuce
300g crayfish tails, cooked
1 pinch cayenne pepper

Food processor
4 serving glasses

1. Cut the avocado in half, remove the stone and scoop the flesh into a food processor. Add the juice of 1 lime and 1 tablespoon of the crème fraîche. Blend until smooth.

2. In a small bowl, mix the mayonnaise, chilli jam and remaining lime juice.

3. Shred the lettuce finely, and place equal amounts in 4 glasses. Divide the avocado mix equally over the lettuce, followed by the crayfish, keeping 4 tails for later.

4. Cover each cocktail with the chilli mayonnaise, and top with a teaspoon of crème fraîche and a crayfish tail. Dust with a pinch of cayenne pepper and serve.

Barolo-Braised Beef with a Root Vegetable Crust

Barolo–Braised Beef with a Root Vegetable Crust

Slow cooking in wine is a sure way to develop tasty, tender meat – and if the wine is a rich Barolo, you get a wonderful depth of flavour. All topped off with a crispy mash, this is a memorable winter warmer for any festive occasion.

Serves 6 50 mins preparation, 3 hours 30 mins cooking

Ingredients
2 tablespoons plain flour
Sea salt and milled black pepper
1.2kg shin of beef, cut into 3cm cubes
5 tablespoons olive oil
2 medium onions, peeled and finely chopped
2 carrots, peeled and finely chopped
2 sticks celery, finely chopped
6 cloves garlic, crushed
1 tablespoon tomato paste
2 bay leaves
1 large sprig thyme
½ litre Barolo wine
½ litre beef stock

For the vegetable crust
500g celeriac, peeled and diced
500g parsnips, peeled and diced
500g potatoes, peeled and diced
100g unsalted butter

To serve
Seasonal green vegetables

Casserole dish
2.5 litre pie dish

1. Pre-heat the oven to 160°C/gas mark 3.

2. Place the flour in a large plastic bag, and season well with salt and pepper. Add the beef, and shake in the flour until evenly coated.

3. Heat a large, heavy-based casserole dish. Add a little olive oil, and sear the beef in batches until browned all over. Remove the beef and keep to one side.

4. In the same casserole dish, add 2 tablespoons of olive oil, and gently fry the onions for 5 minutes. Then add the carrot, celery and garlic, and cook for a further 5 minutes. Stir in the tomato paste and return the beef to the casserole, along with the bay leaves and thyme. Pour over the wine, and bring to the boil.

5. Boil for 2 minutes, then add the stock and bring back to a simmer. Cover the casserole with a lid and transfer to the oven for 2½ to 3 hours, or until the meat is tender.

6. Meanwhile, place the celeriac and parsnips in a large pan. Cover with cold, salted water, bring to the boil and simmer for 20-25 minutes, until tender.

7. Repeat the same process with the potatoes.

8. Drain the vegetables and potatoes, and mash together with a potato ricer or masher. Add two thirds of the butter, mix, and check the seasoning, adding salt if necessary.

9. Remove the casserole from the oven, and increase the temperature to 180°C/gas mark 4. Check the consistency of the cooking liquor. If it's slightly thin, reduce the volume by heating it on the hob. If it's too dry, add a little water.

10. Transfer the casserole to a 2.5 litre pie dish. Cover with the vegetable mash and fluff the top with a fork. Dot the remaining butter over the top, and cook in the oven for 40 minutes, until the top becomes golden.

11. Serve with seasonal green vegetables.

Tiramisu Gateau

Tiramisu Gateau

Tiramisu is such a popular dessert – and when made into a gateau, it adds a real sense of celebration to the proceedings.

Serves 8-10 40 mins preparation, chill overnight

Ingredients

150ml cold, strong black coffee

Vegetable oil to grease

2 large ready-made sponge flan cases

2 eggs, separated

75g caster sugar

1 teaspoon vanilla essence

400g mascarpone cheese

150ml double cream

100ml Tia Maria or Amaretto liqueur

100g milk chocolate, coarsely grated and kept cool

25g chocolate powder

23cm springform cake tin

1. Lightly grease your cake tin, and line with baking parchment.

2. Trim the sponge flans to 23cm, so they fit in the cake tin. Carefully slice through one flan horizontally to make 2 equally thick discs, and then repeat this with the other flan, so you have 4 thin discs.

3. Whisk the egg yolks and 50g of the caster sugar, until light and fluffy. Add the vanilla essence and mascarpone, folding them into the egg mixture.

4. In a separate bowl, whisk the cream until stiff peaks form, and fold this into the mascarpone mixture.

5. In another bowl, whisk the egg whites until you have soft peaks. Gradually whisk in the remaining caster sugar to make a firm meringue, and fold this into the mascarpone mixture.

6. Place a sponge disc, smooth side down into the lined cake tin.

7. Mix the Tia Maria or Amaretto with the cold coffee, and pour a quarter of this evenly over the sponge. Sprinkle with a little grated chocolate, and spread a third of the mascarpone mixture on top.

8. Continue layering in this way, ending with a sponge on the top, soaked in the coffee mixture. Cover the gateau with cling film and chill in the fridge overnight.

9. To serve, remove the gateau from the cake tin and dust with chocolate powder.

Celeriac, Pear and Stilton Soup

This very British flavour combination makes a nice traditional start to our vegetarian menu – and I've introduced a little drama to the way you serve it.

Serves 4 20 mins preparation, 30 mins cooking

Ingredients

30g butter
1 onion, peeled and diced
1 large celeriac, peeled and evenly diced
1 stick celery, washed and diced
1 leek, washed and diced
1 litre water
1 vegetable stock cube

120g Stilton cheese
1 very ripe pear
100ml double cream
Sea salt and milled black pepper

Food processor

1. In a large, heavy-based pan, heat the butter and onion. Cook gently for 5 minutes, stirring occasionally. Add the celeriac, celery and leek, stir and cook for a further 5 minutes.

2. Boil 1 litre of water, and pour it over the stock cube in a jug, whisking until the cube dissolves. Pour the stock into the pan of vegetables, bring to the boil and simmer for 15 minutes, or until the celeriac is tender.

3. Meanwhile, cut 12 small, even cubes out of the Stilton. Keep these to one side, and add the rest to the soup.

4. Peel and core the pear, and cut one quarter into 8 thin slices and keep to one side. Cut the second quarter into small cubes and keep to one side. Cut the remaining pear into chunks, and add these to the soup.

5. Add the double cream, and bring the soup back to the boil. Blend in a food processor until smooth, and then return to the pan. Bring back to a simmer, but don't let it boil. Check the seasoning, adding salt and pepper if necessary.

6. To serve, arrange 3 cubes of Stilton and 2 slices of pear along with a few of the pear cubes in each of 4 soup bowls. Place these in front of your guests, and pour the soup over.

Celeriac, Pear and Stilton Soup

Wild Mushroom, Chestnut and Artichoke Parcels with Thyme and Port Gravy

I think the sign of a good vegetarian dish is when meat eaters don't notice there's anything missing. This is one of those recipes – satisfyingly full of flavour.

Serves 4 40 mins preparation, 25 mins cooking, 1 hour chilling

Ingredients
250g mixed wild mushrooms
2 tablespoons olive oil
4 shallots, finely sliced
2 garlic cloves, crushed
2 tablespoons balsamic vinegar
100g cooked chestnuts, peeled
150ml crème fraîche
100g spinach leaves
200g artichoke hearts
1 teaspoon fresh thyme, chopped
½ teaspoon smoked paprika
Juice of ½ lemon
Sea salt and milled black pepper
100g unsalted butter
1 box filo pastry

For the gravy
2 tablespoons olive oil
50g carrot, peeled and chopped
50g leek, peeled and chopped
50g onion, peeled and chopped
50g celery, peeled and chopped
250ml red wine
500ml vegetable stock
150ml port
1 tablespoon redcurrant jelly
1 teaspoon fresh thyme, picked

To serve
Creamed celeriac (See page 45 for my recipe)

Baking tray, greased

1. Fill a large bowl with cold water, and carefully wash the mushrooms. Place on kitchen paper and pat dry. Roughly cut up the larger ones, so you have evenly sized pieces of mushroom.

2. Heat the olive oil in a frying pan, and add the shallots. Cook for 4 minutes until they soften. Add the garlic and mushrooms, and cook for another 4-5 minutes.

3. Add the vinegar, cook for a minute to reduce the volume, and add the chestnuts and crème fraîche. Cook for a further 10 minutes, and transfer to a bowl to cool.

4. In a pan of boiling water, plunge the spinach leaves for 2 seconds. Drain, and refresh with cold water. Dry on kitchen paper.

Wild Mushroom, Chestnut and Artichoke Parcels with Thyme and Port Gravy

5. Drain the artichokes, cut in half, and add to the mushroom mixture. Add the thyme, paprika and lemon juice, and season with salt and pepper. Chill the mixture in the fridge for 1 hour.

6. Melt the butter gently in a pan or microwave.

7. Working quickly, unroll a sheet of filo pastry, brush with butter and lay another on top. Spread a quarter of the spinach evenly over one half of the filo pastry. Place a quarter of the mushroom stuffing on top of the spinach leaves.

8. Carefully roll the pastry around the filling, folding the edges underneath with a dab of butter to seal it into a parcel.

9. Place the parcel on a greased baking tray, and repeat the process until you have 4 parcels. Keep in the fridge until you're ready to cook them.

To cook the parcels

1. Pre-heat the oven to 180°C/gas mark 4.

2. Remove the parcels from the fridge. Brush with a little melted butter, and bake in the oven for 20-25 minutes, until golden and crisp.

To make the gravy

1. Heat a saucepan, add the olive oil and chopped vegetables, and cook for 3-4 minutes.

2. Add the red wine, bring to the boil and reduce the volume by half.

3. Add the vegetable stock, bring back to the boil and cook for 20 minutes.

4. Pass the gravy through a fine sieve into a bowl.

5. Heat another saucepan, add the port and reduce the volume by half. Add the gravy and redcurrant jelly, and reduce until syrupy. Finally, add the thyme.

To serve

1. Place a parcel on each plate with a drizzle of the gravy down one side. This dish goes really well with creamed celeriac.

Orange Crème Caramel

Freshening up a classic crème caramel with citrus fruit creates a distinctive, memorable dessert – a fitting finale for your festive entertaining.

Serves 8 25 mins preparation, 20 mins cooking, 6 hours chilling

Ingredients

400g caster sugar
45ml water
5 large oranges
2 eggs
14 egg yolks
1 pink grapefruit

1 red grapefruit
8 sprigs mint

8 x 175ml metal pudding basins
Deep roasting tin

1. Pre-heat the oven to 160°C/gas mark 3.

2. Place 8 metal pudding basins in a deep roasting tin, and bring a kettle of water to the boil.

3. Meanwhile, place 100g of the sugar and 45ml of cold water into a very clean, heavy-based saucepan. Put this on a low heat, until the sugar dissolves, and then increase the heat to high. Let the syrup boil, until it turns a golden colour. Remove from the heat, and pour carefully into the base of each mould, twisting to coat the bottom and slightly up the sides.

4. Grate the zest of 2 oranges. Squeeze the juice from 4, measuring 400ml into a saucepan. Add the zest and the remaining 300g of caster sugar, and bring this to the boil over a low heat, stirring until the sugar dissolves. Simmer gently for 2 minutes.

5. Place the eggs and yolks in a large bowl. Whisk together and, while still whisking, slowly pour in the orange mixture. Pass through a fine sieve into a large jug.

6. Pour the mixture equally into each mould.

7. Pour the boiling water into the tray around the moulds, so it comes two thirds of the way up their sides.

8. Bake the crème caramels for 20 minutes, then remove from the oven and leave in the water to cool. Chill in the fridge for at least 6 hours.

9. Peel the grapefruits and remaining orange, and cut into segments.

10. Pour some boiling water into a bowl. Dip one mould into the hot water for 2 seconds to loosen, then press the edges gently to release the crème caramel onto a plate. Repeat this with the remaining caramels, and arrange the citrus segments around each one. Serve with a sprig of mint.

Orange Crème Caramel

Boxing Day Leftovers

Nobody likes to waste food – especially when it's so easy to turn leftovers into some really delicious dishes. I hope these recipes inspire you to transform spare ingredients into special meals with a distinctively festive flavour.

Bubble and Squeak

Bubble and Squeak

As long as Brussels sprouts remain on the Christmas Day menu, bubble and squeak will always be the favourite festive leftover dish – for lunch, supper, or a snack in between.

Serves 4 35 mins preparation, 15 mins cooking

Ingredients
1kg King Edward or good mashing potatoes, peeled and evenly chopped
1 good pinch sea salt
40g butter
5 tablespoons olive oil
1 onion, peeled and finely diced
400g leftover Brussels sprouts
Sea salt and milled black pepper
50g plain flour

To serve
Leftover meats, such as turkey, ham or smoked salmon
Rocket
Crème fraîche

Baking sheet

1. Place the potatoes in a large pan, cover with water and add a good pinch of salt. Bring to the boil and simmer for 15-20 minutes until tender. Drain well, return to the pan and cook for a further 1-2 minutes over a low heat to dry out. Mash the potatoes and mix in the butter. Keep to one side.

2. Pre-heat the oven to 190°C/gas mark 5.

3. Add 1 tablespoon of olive oil to a large frying pan, add the onion and cook on a medium heat for 5 minutes. Add this to the mashed potatoes.

4. Cut the leftover sprouts into quarters and add to the mash. Mix everything together, season with salt and pepper, and shape into 8 round cakes.

5. Pour the flour onto a plate and lightly roll the cakes in it, tapping away any excess.

6. In a large frying pan, add the remaining olive oil and fry the cakes in 2 batches for 3-4 minutes on each side, until golden. Place on a baking sheet.

7. Bake for 10-15 minutes, and serve with other leftovers, such as turkey, ham or smoked salmon, with rocket and crème fraîche.

Turkey and Mango Curry

Turkey and Mango Curry

Okay, I know people joke about turkey curry on Boxing Day – but here we have a creamy, fragrant Thai version, with just enough spicy heat to keep out the winter chill.

Serves 4-6 15 mins preparation, 25 mins cooking

Ingredients
2 tablespoons vegetable oil
1 large onion, peeled and finely chopped
2 cloves garlic, crushed
5cm piece of ginger, peeled and finely diced
1 green pepper, finely diced
2 red chillies, de-seeded and finely diced
½ stick lemongrass, finely shredded
2 tablespoons Thai green curry paste
450ml coconut milk
250ml water
1 chicken stock cube
300g cooked turkey, diced
Sea salt and milled black pepper
1 mango, peeled and diced
3 tablespoons fresh coriander

To serve
Sticky rice

1. Heat a large frying pan, add the vegetable oil and onion, and cook gently for 5 minutes.

2. Increase the heat and add the garlic, ginger, green pepper, chillies and lemongrass. Keep stirring, and cook for 3-4 minutes.

3. Add the Thai curry paste, and cook for a further 2 minutes.

4. Stir in the coconut milk and water, and crumble in the stock cube. Bring to the boil and simmer for 5 minutes.

5. Add the turkey and simmer gently for 10-12 minutes.

6. Check the seasoning, adding salt and pepper if necessary.

7. Place the mango on top, sprinkle with coriander and serve with sticky rice.

Smoked Salmon and Broccoli Tagliatelle

Due to its intense flavour, a little smoked salmon goes a long way. With this dish, nobody would guess you're using up leftovers.

Serves 4 20 mins preparation, 15 mins cooking

Ingredients

250g broccoli
Sea salt and milled black pepper
1 pinch saffron (optional)
2 tablespoons olive oil
2 shallots, finely chopped
50ml white wine

150ml whipping cream
200g smoked salmon trimmings, cut into ribbons
400g dried tagliatelle
Juice of ½ lemon

1. Bring a large pan of salted water to the boil. Cut the broccoli into small florets and boil for 2 minutes. Drain, and then refresh in cold water.

2. If you're using the saffron, place in a small cup with 3 tablespoons of boiling water to soften.

3. Heat 1 tablespoon of olive oil in a large saucepan. Add the shallots and cook for 5 minutes until soft.

4. Add the white wine, saffron and cream. Bring to the boil, and simmer for 10 minutes to thicken slightly. Add half of the salmon trimmings, and leave to stand off the heat to let the flavours infuse.

5. Bring a large pan of salted water to the boil. Add 1 tablespoon of olive oil and put the pasta in the pan. Cook for 10-12 minutes, or according to the packet instructions, until tender.

6. Add the broccoli to the pasta for the final 2 minutes of cooking, and then strain in a colander.

7. Re-heat the sauce, add the lemon juice, and pour in the pasta and broccoli. Mix to coat the pasta, and divide between 4 plates.

8. Scatter the remaining ribbons of smoked salmon on the top of each one, and serve with a twist of black pepper.

Smoked Salmon and Broccoli Tagliatelle

Christmas Pudding Ice Cream

Christmas Pudding Ice Cream

Why eat Christmas pudding only one day a year? Turn it into a rich, creamy ice cream, and you can keep enjoying it for up to a week.

Serves 6-8 30 mins preparation, plus freezing

Ingredients
200g leftover Christmas pudding
3-4 tablespoons rum
400ml whipping cream
4 egg yolks
100g caster sugar
150g Greek plain yogurt

1. Roughly crumble the leftover Christmas pudding into a bowl, and add the rum.

2. In a saucepan, bring 300ml of the whipping cream to the boil, then remove from the heat.

3. Whisk the egg yolks and sugar until light and creamy.

4. Pour a third of the hot cream over the eggs, whisking at the same time, and then add the rest. Pour the mixture into the pan, and stir continuously over a low heat until it thickens slightly and coats the back of a spoon.

5. Add the cream and egg mixture to the Christmas pudding crumbs to make a custard, and leave to cool completely.

6. Whisk the remaining 100ml of whipping cream until it has firm peaks. Add this to the cold custard, along with the Greek yogurt. Using a whisk, gently fold everything together, and then pour into a plastic container with a lid.

7. Put in the freezer, and stir every 45 minutes until it sets – this will stop the pudding sinking to the bottom.

8. The ice cream will keep in the freezer for up to a week.

Parties and New Year's Eve

If you're hosting a festive get-together, and want some inspiration for canapés and nibbles, you'll find a variety of ideas over the next few pages – plus all the drinks recipes you need to get the party started!

Mini Black Pudding Scotch Eggs

Mini Black Pudding Scotch Eggs

Serve these up at any festive get-together, and you'll make yourself extremely popular. The humble Scotch egg will never be the same again!

Makes 12 30 mins preparation, 5 mins cooking, 15 mins chilling

Ingredients

12 quail eggs

1 tablespoon malt vinegar

250g soft black pudding (avoid firm, rubbery ones)

30g plain flour, seasoned with sea salt and milled black pepper

1 egg, beaten

100g breadcrumbs

1-2 litres rapeseed oil

Fryer or large pan

Food thermometer

1. Bring a small pan of water to the boil. Carefully add 6 of the quail eggs, bring back to the boil and cook for 1½ minutes. Using a slotted spoon, carefully lift out the eggs and plunge them into a bowl of cold water. Repeat with the other 6 eggs.

2. Drain and refill with cold water, add the vinegar, and leave to chill in the fridge for 15 minutes – this helps to soften the egg shells.

3. Take one of the eggs and tap it gently on a work surface to crack the shell. Then, using the palm of your hand, roll it lightly to crack the shell further, and pick the shell away.

4. Repeat this with the rest of the eggs. Dip in cold water to remove any bits of remaining shell, and place on a sheet of kitchen roll.

5. Remove any casing from the black pudding, and put in a bowl. Squeeze between your fingers to soften it.

6. Wash your hands and, keeping them slightly wet, take a ball of black pudding about twice the size of the quail egg. Pat in your palm to flatten, and then place an egg in the centre. Bring the edges around to cover the egg evenly with the black pudding. Repeat this process with all 12 eggs.

7. Roll each Scotch egg in the seasoned flour, then dip in the beaten egg and roll in the breadcrumbs. Keep covered in the fridge until you need them.

8. In an electric deep fryer or large pan, heat the oil to 170°C. Cook the Scotch eggs in 2 batches, for 4-5 minutes until crisp and golden.

Marinated Bocconcini

Makes 24 15 mins preparation

Ingredients

1 red chilli, de-seeded and finely chopped
1 tablespoon fresh mint, finely chopped
1 spring onion, finely chopped
Juice and grated zest of 1 lemon
4 tablespoons olive oil

Sea salt and milled black pepper
24 small Bocconcini mozzarella balls
6 slices Parma ham

24 cocktail sticks

1. Mix the chilli, mint, spring onion, lemon juice and zest with the olive oil, and season with a little salt and pepper. Add the mozzarella balls and marinate for 10 minutes.

2. Cut each slice of Parma ham into 4 strips, roll each strip around a marinated mozzarella ball, and secure with a cocktail stick.

3. Drizzle a little marinade over the top to serve.

Pesto Palmiers

Makes 24 20 mins preparation, 15 mins cooking, 10 mins chilling

Ingredients

200g ready-made puff pastry
1 tablespoon plain flour to dust
3 tablespoons pesto
50g Parmesan cheese, freshly grated

Milled black pepper
Sea salt

Large baking tray

1. Pre-heat the oven to 190°C/gas mark 5.

2. Roll out the pastry on a lightly floured surface, into a rectangle about 30cm x 20cm. Trim the edges if necessary.

3. Spread the pesto thinly over the pastry. Sprinkle the Parmesan evenly on top, and season with a little black pepper.

4. Roll the pastry from both long ends to the centre, to make 2 spirals that meet in the middle. Chill in the freezer for 10 minutes, to make it firm.

5. Cut the joined rolls across in 1cm slices. Arrange these on a large baking tray, with space in between to let them spread. Sprinkle with a little sea salt, and bake for 15 minutes until golden and crisp.

6. Transfer the palmiers to a wire rack to cool.

7. Serve while still warm – or cool completely, store in an airtight container and warm through before serving. They'll keep for 2-3 days.

Marinated Bocconcini and Pesto Palmiers

Smoked Salmon Blinis and Tequila Prawns with Parma Ham

Smoked Salmon Blinis

Makes 32 15 mins preparation

Ingredients

2 x 135g packs of blinis
150g crème fraîche
Juice and grated zest of 1 lemon
1 tablespoon creamed horseradish sauce

Sea salt and milled black pepper
200g smoked salmon, sliced
100g pot of salmon caviar (optional)
4 sprigs dill or chervil, chopped

1. Pre-heat the oven to 160°C/gas mark 3.

2. Wrap the blinis loosely in tin foil, and bake for 4-5 minutes until warm.

3. Mix the crème fraîche, lemon zest and horseradish, and season with a little salt and pepper.

4. Cut the slices of smoked salmon into 2cm-thick ribbons.

5. Place a teaspoon of crème fraîche on each blini, followed by a twist of smoked salmon. Season with a little more black pepper and a splash of lemon juice. Decorate with a pinch of salmon caviar, if you're using it, and the dill or chervil. Serve on a platter.

Tequila Prawns with Parma Ham

Makes 24 30 mins preparation, 5 mins cooking, 15 mins chilling

Ingredients

24 raw king prawns, peeled
6 slices Parma ham, each sliced into 4 strips
3 tablespoons olive oil
1 pinch chilli flakes
2 cloves garlic, crushed
Juice and grated zest of 2 limes
4 tablespoons tequila

For the garlic mayonnaise

150g good-quality mayonnaise
3 cloves garlic, crushed
Juice of ½ lemon
1 pinch paprika, plus extra to serve
Sea salt and milled black pepper

1. Mix all the garlic mayonnaise ingredients together, and season with salt and pepper.

2. Place in a small serving dish, and sprinkle a little paprika on top.

To cook the prawns and serve

1. Wrap each king prawn tightly in a strip of Parma ham.

2. Heat the olive oil in a large frying pan. Add the chilli, garlic, and lime zest, then the prawns. Cook for 2 minutes on each side.

3. Add the tequila and lime juice, and cook for a few more seconds.

4. Take the pan off the heat, and give the prawns a good toss in the cooking juices. Transfer to a serving dish, and serve with the garlic mayonnaise.

Mini Lemon and Raspberry Tartlets with Poinsettia

Mini Lemon and Raspberry Tartlets

Maximum taste and indulgence for minimum effort – the speed and simplicity of this recipe leaves you time to enjoy the party as much as your guests.

Makes 24 15 mins preparation

Ingredients
3 tablespoons lemon curd
100ml ready-made custard
100ml double cream
24-pack of mini croustades
24 fresh raspberries
1 dessertspoon icing sugar

1. Mix the lemon curd and custard together.

2. Whisk the double cream to soft peaks and fold into the custard mix.

3. Divide the mixture between the croustades, top each one with a raspberry and dust with icing sugar.

Poinsettia

Named after the popular bright-red Christmas flowering plant, this simple cocktail makes a refreshing festive aperitif.

Serves 6-8 5 mins preparation

Ingredients
750ml bottle Prosecco or other sparkling
wine, well chilled
125ml Cointreau
500ml cranberry juice, ice cold

1. Pour the Prosecco into a large jug.

2. Add the Cointreau and cranberry juice.

3. Stir, and pour into champagne flutes.

Christmas Pudding Vodka

They say you can flavour vodka with anything – and this recipe proves it, packing in all the festive fruits and spices.

Makes 1 bottle 10 mins preparation, 1 week marinating

Ingredients

2 cinnamon sticks
4 cloves
2 pieces of blade mace
100g mixed peel
1 x 700ml bottle vodka (keeping the bottle and cap)
200g light muscovado sugar
150g raisins

200g sultanas
Juice and grated zest of 1 orange
Juice and grated zest of 1 lemon
2 teaspoons mixed spice

Large bowl or Kilner jar
Funnel
Coffee-filter paper

1. Sterilise the Kilner jar by submerging it in a large container of boiling water for 2 minutes. Take it out and dry. Alternatively, run through your dishwasher on a full cycle.

2. In a dry frying pan, warm through the cinnamon sticks, cloves and mace for 2 minutes, being careful not to burn them. Take the pan off the heat, and add the mixed peel to warm through.

3. Place these warm ingredients in a large bowl or sterilised Kilner jar. Add all the remaining ingredients, and give them a good stir. Remember to keep the vodka bottle and cap.

4. Seal the jar, or if you're using a bowl, cover with cling film. Store in a cool place for a week, stirring the mixture every day.

5. After a week, strain the mixture through a fine sieve into a large bowl or jug, pressing down well to extract as much liquid as possible. Keep the fruits, and discard the mace, cinnamon and cloves.

6. Place a funnel lined with a coffee-filter paper in the top of the vodka bottle, and pour the liquid through. Seal with the cap and keep in the fridge – it should last for up to 6 months. Or you can keep it in the freezer, and serve super-cold from there.

You could add the vodka-soaked fruits you've saved to the Christmas pudding ice cream recipe on page 80. Or simply serve them with vanilla ice cream.

Christmas Pudding Vodka

Egg Nog

Serves 8 20 mins preparation

Ingredients

3 large eggs, separated
100g caster sugar
600ml whole milk
¼ teaspoon vanilla extract
100ml rum or bourbon

100ml whipping cream
½ teaspoon fresh nutmeg, grated

Punch glasses

1. Place the egg yolks and caster sugar in a bowl, and whisk until thick and creamy.

2. Heat the milk in a saucepan until it's almost boiling. Remove from the heat and pour one third onto the egg yolks, whisking as you go. Keep whisking and add the remaining milk.

3. Pour the mixture back into the pan and heat gently, stirring with a wooden spoon until it's smooth and slightly thickened. Take off the heat and pour into a large bowl. Add the vanilla extract and rum or bourbon to make a custard, and leave to cool.

4. In a separate bowl, beat the egg whites until they form soft peaks.

5. In another bowl, beat the whipping cream – again, to form soft peaks.

6. Fold the cream into the custard mixture, followed by the egg whites.

7. Chill the egg nog in the fridge until you're ready to serve, and then ladle into punch glasses and sprinkle with grated nutmeg.

Reindeer Caesar

Serves 1 5 mins preparation

Ingredients

30ml vodka
150ml Clamato juice
2 teaspoons lemon juice
1 dash Tabasco sauce
1 dash Worcestershire sauce
1 pinch sea salt
1 pinch nutmeg, grated
Ice cubes

1. Pour all the ingredients, apart from the nutmeg and ice cubes, into a highball glass.

2. Add the ice cubes, and mix well.

3. Sprinkle with grated nutmeg to serve.

Shirley Temple and Mulled Cider

Shirley Temple

Legend has it this 'mocktail' was invented in the 1930s for child actress Shirley Temple. It's still popular today, with kids and adults alike.

Serves 1 5 mins preparation

Ingredients
Ice cubes
90ml fresh orange juice
180ml ginger ale
20ml grenadine
1 maraschino cherry

1. Fill a highball glass two thirds with ice.

2. Add the orange juice, and then the ginger ale, followed by the grenadine.

3. Finally, pop the cherry on top.

Mulled Cider

Serves 10-12 10 mins preparation, 20 mins cooking

Ingredients
2 litres unfiltered cider (cloudy)
1 apple
12 cloves
6 cinnamon sticks
Juice and peel of 1 orange
100g soft brown sugar
3cm piece of fresh ginger, cut into
thick slices
4 allspice berries

1. Pour the cider into a large saucepan.

2. Stud the apple with cloves, and add this to the cider with the remaining ingredients.

3. Bring to the boil, reduce the heat and simmer gently for 20 minutes.

4. Strain the mulled cider through a fine sieve, and serve hot with half a cinnamon stick in each glass.

Lamona Appliance, Sink and Tap Collection

The Lamona range is exclusive to Howdens Joinery and has been selected to perfectly complement our range of kitchens.

Lamona appliances are designed to look great and are manufactured to the highest standards to ensure they are durable and reliable, use less energy and water, and run quietly, whilst providing excellent value for money.

You can choose from ovens, microwaves, hobs, extractors, fridges, freezers, dishwashers, tumble dryers, sinks and taps, which are all designed to fit beautifully in your Howdens kitchen.

All Lamona appliances come with a 2 year manufacturer's guarantee and a 5 year guarantee on oven door glass, and what we believe is the best after sales service in the UK.

You will have the reassurance that last year we supplied 600,000 appliances and 550,000 sinks and taps to UK homes.

Lamona is available from stock in over 540 local depots to your trade professional. To find out more and for detailed product specifications, please refer to **www.lamona.co.uk**

Tewkesbury Stone Kitchen

Lamona Double Fan Oven and Lamona Professional 5 Burner Gas Hob

Lamona Windermere 1.5 Bowl Sink and Lamona Chrome Victorian
Swan Neck Monobloc Tap

99

The General Tarleton

An old coaching inn with contemporary comforts, The General Tarleton Inn is in the pretty village of Ferrensby close to both York and Harrogate. Owned and run by John and Claire Topham for the past 12 years, The General Tarleton is constantly evolving but always sticks to the basic philosophy of offering great service and excellent food and drink in a relaxed atmosphere, and if you are staying the night, a comfortable room to rest your head.

The focus is on food

In The General Tarleton kitchen, John heads an experienced and dedicated team. Menus change daily to reflect the seasons and the pick of the catch or crop that day. John gets a call most days from the fishing boats as they return to port and within hours the fish is in the kitchen. Yorkshire has an abundance of excellent suppliers which The General Tarleton has worked with over the years to obtain the very best seasonal produce.

The General Tarleton Inn, Boroughbridge Road, Ferrensby, Knaresborough, HG5 0PZ
Tel 01423 340284 www.generaltarleton.co.uk